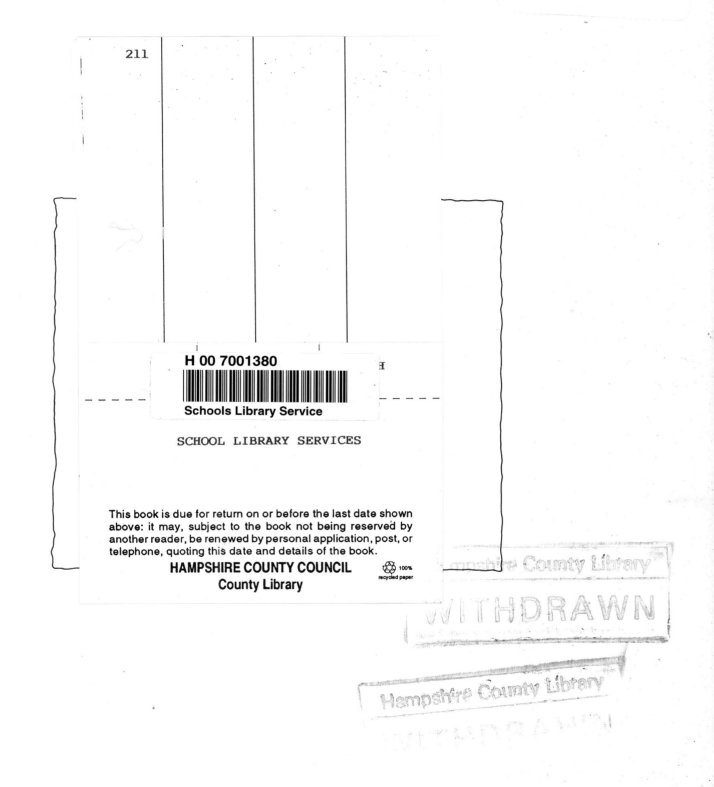

About the author

Vivian French lives in Bristol, in the
south-west of England. Every spring when her
daughters were little they visited the pond next door
to collect some frogspawn, bring it home,
and watch the tadpoles hatch.
Her cat was always VERY interested.
Now that her children are grown up, Vivian
travels about, telling stories and writing books.
"A Song for Little Toad" was shortlisted
for the Smarties Book Prize.

About the illustrator

Alison Bartlett also lives in Bristol,
with her son Joel and two Jack Russell terriers.
She has illustrated several books by Vivian French,
including "Oliver's Vegetables", which was recommended
for the National Art Library Illustration Awards.
Before she painted the pictures for this book
Alison thought frogspawn was "disgusting" —
now she thinks it's amazing.

For Jane Slade
V.F.

For Rebecca, with much love
A.B.

Consultant: Martin Jenkins

First published 2000 by Walker Books Ltd
87 Vauxhall Walk, London SE11 5HJ

This edition published 2001

2   4   6   8   10   9   7   5   3   1

Text © 2000 Vivian French
Illustrations © 2000 Alison Bartlett

This book has been typeset in Tapioca.

Printed in Hong Kong

British Library Cataloguing in Publication Data:
a catalogue record for this book is available
from the British Library.

ISBN 0-7445-7819-1

Growing Frogs

Vivian French   illustrated by Alison Bartlett

WALKER BOOKS
AND SUBSIDIARIES
LONDON • BOSTON • SYDNEY

Once, when I was little, my mum
read me a story about a frog that
drank and drank and drank,
and grew **bigger**
and **bigger**
and **bigger.**

Afterwards Mum asked me if I'd like
to watch some real frogs growing.

"I know where there's a pond with lots
of frogs' eggs in it," she said. "We could
bring some home."

I was frightened.
"I don't want any
frogs jumping about
getting bigger
and **bigger**
and **bigger**," I said.

But Mum gave me a hug. "It's only a story,"
she said. "Even when our frogs are grown up
they'll still be smaller than my hand."

"Oh," I said. "OK."

Next day we went
to look at the pond.
The water was dark
brown, and there
was grey jelly stuff
floating on the top.

"Yuck!" I said.

"There's the frogspawn," said Mum.
And she pointed to the grey jelly stuff.
"I bet that was laid last Friday night.
The frogs were croaking so loudly,
I couldn't get to sleep."

Male frogs croak to attract female frogs
for mating. The females lay eggs called frogspawn.

"You see the black dot in the
middle of each jelly shell?" said Mum.
"That's going to grow into a tadpole."

"Where are the frogs?" I asked.
"Tadpoles grow into frogs," she said.
"Little ones — no giant frogs here!"

Mum put some pondweed
and some stones into a bag.
She filled a bucket with
pond water, then I scooped
a little of the frogspawn
into it.

Always use pond water for growing frogs at home.
Tap water has chemicals like fluoride in it,
which might poison them.

11

When we got
home we put everything
into a big fish tank in
the kitchen.

The cat kept
peering at it, so
we had to put
a wire net over
the top.

I counted
twenty-seven
little black dots.
Each dot was inside
its own jelly shell.

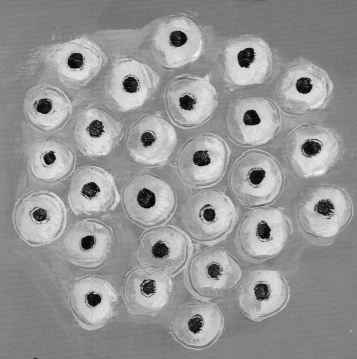

The tank needs to be somewhere that's cool and away from direct sunlight.

13

Every day when I woke up
I went straight downstairs
to look at the frogspawn.

The little dots
grew into bigger dots,

and then into
tiny commas.

In a tank, the eggs hatch into tadpoles
about ten days after they are laid.

And one morning
I saw the first tadpole
wriggling out of its
jelly shell!

At first the tadpoles didn't do much.
They just stayed close to their jelly shells
and nibbled at the pondweed.

But after two or three days
they looked quite different. There
were feathery things on their heads
and I could see their eyes.

The feathery bits are called gills and they're
what underwater animals use for breathing.

They swam **very** fast.

Ten of the eggs
didn't hatch out.
The black dots went
dull and cloudy,
and Mum took
them away.

Then we cleaned out
the tank and put in fresh
weed and pond water.
   One of the tadpoles swam
into my hand when I was
putting a stone back.
It was slippery and slithery,
and it made me jump.

After the tadpoles hatch,
the pond water needs
to be changed at least
twice a week.

After a bit I got used to having tadpoles
and I didn't look at them so often.

When Mum told me their little feathery bits
had gone I didn't believe her.

But it was **true.**

Tadpoles only have gills outside their bodies at first.
Then they grow gills inside their bodies
and the outside ones disappear.

It was me that saw the next change, though.

"Look!"

I shouted, and Mum rushed to see.
Some of the tadpoles had grown two
little bumps. Mum said the bumps
would grow into back legs.

They grew very quickly.

One day there were
two little bumps.

The next day the
bumps were stumps.

The day after that they were almost proper legs.

And when the feet unfolded they were webbed, like tiny browny-green fans.

"They aren't tadpoles any more," I said.
"They're not-quite-frogs."

The not-quite-frogs grew front legs next.

And then their tails got shorter

and their mouths got **wider**.

"Now they're frogs," Mum said.
"Baby ones."

Soon the baby frogs were popping up and gulping at the surface of the water.

One of them tried to climb on to the stones, but it slid off. Mum said they were getting ready to leave the water.

"Grown-up frogs breathe air," she said. "That's what the stones are for — so our frogs can climb out of the water and breathe."

As tadpoles slowly turn into frogs, they grow lungs for breathing air and their gills disappear.

Not long after that Mum said it was time to take our baby frogs back to live in the pond with all the other baby frogs.

I was sorry to leave them, but Mum said we could come back and visit every day.

Baby frogs need space to grow and room to hop around. Grown-up frogs live most of their lives on land, only returning to their ponds to breed.

One rainy morning a week later
Mum woke me up very early.

"Hurry!" she said, and we ran downstairs
and out to the pond.

There were hundreds of tiny
frogs hopping over the grass.

"They're looking for dark wet places to
live in," Mum said. "But they won't go far,
and in a couple of years they'll be back
to lay frogspawn of their own."

"Will they be bigger then?" I asked.

"Just a little," said Mum.

"Good," I said. "I like
having frogs jumping about
getting bigger
and bigger
and bigger!"

Index

croaking 9

eggs 7, 9, 18

frogspawn 9, 14–15, 29

gills 17, 20, 26

hatching 14–15, 18, 19

legs 21–24

mating 9

pond 8–9, 27, 28

tadpoles 10, 15–17, 19, 20, 23

tank 12, 13, 19

Look up the pages to find out about
all these froggy things.
Don't forget to look at both kinds of word —
this kind and *this kind.*

Frogs are in danger — please help!

Rules for frog-lovers

⊙ Don't ever take frogspawn from a wild pond.

⊙ If you take frogspawn from a garden pond, only take a LITTLE.

⊙ Always take your frogs back to the pond they came from.

NOTES FOR TEACHERS

The READ AND WONDER series is an innovative and versatile resource for reading, thinking and discovery. Each book invites children to become excited about a topic, see how varied information books can be, and want to find out more.

👉 **Reading aloud** The story form makes these books ideal for reading aloud – in their own right or as part of a cross-curricular topic, to a child or to a whole class. After you've introduced children to the books in this way, they can revisit and enjoy them again and again.

👉 **Shared reading** Big Book editions are available for several titles, so children can read along, discuss the topic, and comment on the different ways information is presented – to wonder together.

👉 **Group and guided reading** Children need to experience a range of reading materials. Information books like these help develop the skills of reading to learn, as part of learning to read. With the support of a reading group, children can become confident, flexible readers.

👉 **Paired reading** It's fun to take turns to read the information in the main text or captions. With a partner, children can explore the pages to satisfy their curiosity and build their understanding.

👉 **Individual reading** These books can be read for interest and pleasure by children at home and in school.

👉 **Research** Once children have been introduced to these books through reading aloud, they can use them for independent or group research, as part of a curricular topic.

👉 **Children's own writing** You can offer these books as strong models for children's own information writing. They can record their observations and findings about a topic, make field notes and sketches, and add extra snippets of information for the reader.

Above all, Read and Wonders are to be enjoyed, and encourage children to develop a lasting curiosity about the world they live in.

Sue Ellis, Centre for Language in Primary Education